"This ma America's
most gif packs the
statemen sake he
[Jesus] showing
the histo of Jesus
Christ for us human beings, who are mired and lost in sin. In simple yet profound and pungent prose, we hear again, in Professor Wellum's words, the truth of this ancient statement. Highly recommended."

Michael A. G. Haykin, Professor of Church History and Biblical Spirituality, The Southern Baptist Theological Seminary, Louisville, Kentucky

"Knowing *why* Christ died and rose again helps us see our needs more clearly. Knowing *what* Christ has completed in his work helps us live more assuredly. Knowing *who* Christ is in himself anchors our hope more solidly. Stephen Wellum has given the church a clear and winsome picture of the why, what, and who of the atonement, a doctrine that brings confidence and connection to the hearts of Christ's people."

Mason King, Executive Director of Discipleship, The Village Church, Flower Mound, Texas

"Steve Wellum exults in the glorious reality that Christ saves sinners as the supreme prophet, priest, and king."

Andy Naselli, Professor of Systematic Theology and New Testament, Bethlehem College and Seminary, Minneapolis, Minnesota

"A beautiful and compact explanation of what Christ achieved in his death and resurrection. This work will cause you to worship God in Christ for what was accomplished in Jesus' ministry, where he came as our prophet, priest, and king."

Thomas R. Schreiner, author, *The King in His Beauty*

"Stephen Wellum offers a clear, compelling, and biblical exploration of Christ's finished work on the cross. Rooted in Scripture and framed through Christ's threefold office as prophet, priest, and king, this book powerfully demonstrates why Jesus alone is the all-sufficient Saviour. This is a small book about a grand topic, and I hope that for many it is an entry point to a lifetime of exploring the glory of the cross."

Jeremy Treat, Pastor for Preaching and Vision, Reality LA, Los Angeles, California, and author of *The Crucified King*

Union

It Is Finished

Stephen Wellum

It Is Finished

www.UnionPublishing.org
Bridgend, Wales, United Kingdom

Cover and layout design by somethingmorecreative.com

978-1-7384324-8-6 (paperback)

978-1-7384324-9-3 (eBook)

Contents

Essentials Series Preface

Very simply, this series introduces the essential, non-negotiable truths of the gospel.

And what are they? This is how the apostle Paul speaks of the gospel in the opening sentence of his letter to the Romans:

> Paul, a servant of Christ Jesus, called to be an apostle, set apart for the gospel of God, which he promised beforehand through his prophets in the holy Scriptures, concerning his Son, who was descended from David according to the flesh and was declared to be the Son of God in power according to the Spirit of holiness by his resurrection from the dead, Jesus Christ our Lord. (Rom. 1:1–4)

For Paul, the gospel is a God-centred message: it is "the gospel of God." It is a Trinitarian message: the Father revealing his Son in the power of the Spirit. It is a biblical message: proclaimed "in the holy Scriptures." It concerns Christ, the Son of God, and his work of redemption. And it is a message made effective in the regenerating power of the Spirit. In other words, the Christian gospel is good news concerning the Father, the Son, and the Spirit, and the work of the Father, the Son, and the Spirit, in revelation, redemption, and regeneration.[1]

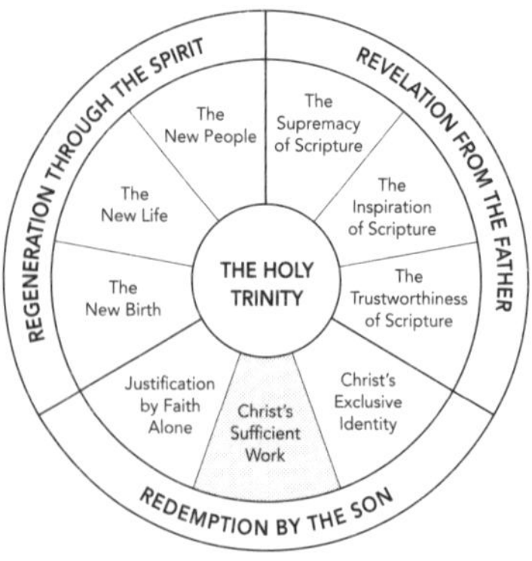

1 This diagram was first used and explained in Michael Reeves, *Gospel People: A Call for Evangelical Integrity* (Wheaton, IL: Crossway, 2022), 20, 119.

These truths are all interconnected, and together they make up our beautiful, biblical, Trinitarian, Christ-centred, and Spirit-effected good news. This series will introduce, and refresh readers in, this gospel. Ten short books cover the most basic subject areas of the gospel, as shown in the two inner circles of this diagram.

Each book will introduce its own subject area, and yet the aim of this series is not merely to communicate content. The gospel, after all, is not merely revelation. It is a revelation that *redeems* and *regenerates*. And so, may you be renewed as you read, and brought to worship and enjoy "the glory of the blessed God" (1 Tim. 1:11).

Michael Reeves
Series Editor

1

It Is Finished!

If you've ever listened to an Easter sermon, then you may know that one of the seven statements of Jesus as he hung on the cross was the simple but powerful sentence: "It is finished" (John 19:30).

But what exactly was finished? What does the sentence mean? And how and why is it significant today?

Given the horrible context of the crucifixion, Jesus could have been merely signalling the end of his life—a final admission that it was about to be over. Indeed, many onlookers at the time may well have understood those words in this way.

However, this interpretation would be a serious mistake. Scripture teaches us clearly that Jesus' death on the cross was not an accident, nor was it a tragic ending to an incredible life. His death was, in fact, part of God's eternal plan to "save his people from their sins" (Matt. 1:21). Thus, "It is finished" does not signal Jesus' defeat or resignation, but, ironically, his triumph, his accomplishment, and the completion of the work he had come to earth to do (John 17:1–5).

This is why, for Christians, Jesus' cry is decidedly positive: it's good news! For it reminds us that God hasn't left us to save ourselves; instead, he has provided a Saviour for us. And more than that, Jesus is able to meet all our needs. Scripture views Jesus as both the exclusive Saviour and the all-sufficient Saviour, for he alone can save us, and he does so fully and completely.

However, today, unless you know the teaching of Scripture, "it is finished" risks being interpreted as a cry of abject defeat, and all this talk of good news and God's eternal plan will seem at odds with it. For this reason, I want to explain more fully from the Bible why Jesus alone is indeed the exclusive and sufficient Lord and Saviour, uncovering why he is worthy of all of our trust, love, and obedience.

I will do this first by taking a look at the human condition. For unless we know what I will identify as the "bad news"—the true nature of the problem humanity faces—we won't understand why we even need Jesus, let alone the relevance of the "good news" of what he has achieved and won for us. Then we will explore why Jesus alone can save us and meet all our needs, and indeed, why his cry from the cross, "it is finished," is not only good news but the greatest news imaginable for us and for our world.

My goal is to lead you not merely to a deeper knowledge of our Lord Jesus Christ, but to a greater adoration of him. He is not simply a notable person from history; he is the divine Son and living Saviour who wins our very hearts.

2
Our Need for a Saviour

The human condition has been the subject of countless books, films, and songs down through the years. Think of J.R.R. Tolkien's masterful examination of human nature in *The Lord of the Rings*. In this classic book series, he explores the weakness of humans and other creatures that lust after the ring of power. Sadly, if they do get the ring, they often use its power for evil ends.

And the misuse of power is just one way we fail. We don't have to look very far to find evidence of this. In our marriages, families, and lives, we see such brokenness, sadness, and death. Recent news bulletins tell a terrible story: wars and rumours of wars abound, suicide rates soar, and our inhumane treatment of one another is universal. The dust of death is over our entire world. If we're being honest, we have to acknowledge that there's something desperately wrong with us.

But what is the *root* of our problem? How you answer this question depends on your worldview. In society at large, humanity's problem is explained in a variety of ways, and mostly in terms of natural causes. So, for example, some attribute it to a lack of education. If we simply educate people more, then they will be kinder and gentler. Or some think that if people weren't poor but had an equal distribution of money, then everyone would be well and happy. Others blame human evil on our cultural environment. Change society, and that will change the people within it!

However, according to Scripture, all of these explanations and proposed solutions to our problem are too surface-level. They don't go nearly deep enough: the equivalent of applying a small bandage to a severe wound.

If we have a terminal disease, unless we know exactly what it is, we won't know how to treat it correctly. So too, spiritually speaking, unless we grasp the "bad news" about ourselves, we will never see our need of a Saviour and why it is that Jesus alone can save us. In other words, we will never grasp that when Jesus says, "It is finished," this truly is good news that overcomes the bad.

But to understand the Bible's description of and answer to our problem, we need to go right back to the beginning. We must ask some very basic questions:

- Who is God?
- Why did God create us?
- What exactly is wrong with us?

Who is God?

If we're trying to understand ourselves, why start with God? Shouldn't we start with ourselves?

We start with God because God created us. So there's no way to understand who *we* are without understanding who *he* is. In fact, trying to know who we are apart from the

God who designed us is absolutely futile.

From the opening verses of Scripture, we discover that God, and God alone, is eternal—unlike us, he has always existed. He is uncreated—unlike us, nobody created him. And he needs nothing—unlike us, who are highly dependent creatures (see Genesis 1–2).

Think about that for a moment, for it's mind-blowing—God is so very, very different from us. Even before the universe itself existed, God, in all of his perfection, did exist. And he did so as the one true God in perfect fellowship and communion in three persons: Father, Son, and Holy Spirit—also known as the Trinity.[1]

The nature of God as Trinity helps us understand that "God is love" (1 John 4:8). Love is not something God has; it is who he *is* and always *has been*. Even before time began, God was not alone. The eternal Father has always been loving in his shared relation to

1 On the Trinity, see the Series Preface (pp. 7–9 above) as well as the Essentials series volume *The Trinity* (2024) by Donald Fairbairn.

the eternal Son (John 17:24) and the eternal Holy Spirit. There has always been fellowship between Father, Son, and Spirit, who eternally enjoy one another and eternally overflow in their loving relations to each other. God enjoys perfect harmony, unity, and joy without reference to any other being or thing.

What's more, there is no ugliness or unkindness or darkness in God, but perfect peace and purity. He is beautiful: "All his ways are beautifully fatherly."[2] He is the Holy One (Exod. 3:2–5; Isa. 6:1–3). His holiness enables his self-sufficiency, lordship, majesty, and fatherly goodness.

It is for this reason that God can be described as categorically different from us, and consequently why he shares his glory with no one else (Isa. 40:25). It is also why God is perfectly good, and indeed why he is the true standard of righteousness and justice. The God who is love is the God who "cannot look at wrong" (Hab. 1:13). As our

---

2 Michael Reeves, *Delighting in the Trinity: An Introduction to the Christian Faith* (Downers Grove, IL: InterVarsity Press, 2012), 23.

world struggles to know what the standard of goodness is, Scripture reminds us that it is God, and God alone, who is the perfect and absolute standard in himself. God is not fickle, as if he has any need or might change from day to day. And God doesn't depend on us; he is complete within himself. In a humorous statement in the Psalms, God reminds us that if he were hungry, "I would not tell you, for the world and its fullness are mine" (50:12).

Understanding who God is, then, helps us rightly to understand why he created us.

Why did God create us?

If God is already complete in himself, why did he create us? It wasn't because he needed creatures to love him or serve him, for he *is* love and has existed in loving fellowship for eternity.

At its deepest level, God's act of creation was a free choice to share himself in the perfections of his love with us. God is the fountain of goodness, full of life (Ps. 36:9), and amazingly, he has chosen to share his abundant goodness with his creation. In fact, Colossians 1 tell us that all things were created through Christ and *for* Christ (vv. 15–16). God's creation is overwhelmingly beautiful, and this too reflects God's nature. In Genesis 1 we read that time and time again, God looked at what he had made and saw that it was very good—an overflow of his very heart.

Scripture teaches us that God created humans as the pinnacle of his creation. He created us in his "image" and "likeness" (Gen. 1:26), unlike any other creature, and for the purpose of knowing God, loving God, and serving him as his kings and queens over creation. As David reflects on this truth, it leads him to give thanks to God for such a privilege (Psalm 8). Humans are not evolved animals, but royalty created to be in covenant relationship with God and to be rulers over his world. Truly, this is something to celebrate and enjoy!

What's more, in creation God was present with his people, for he walked among them (Gen. 3:8). He gave them a place to inhabit

(2:8) and a world to work within, fill, and have dominion over (1:28). They were fully known and fully loved, savouring the one who is life. They lived under his good and gracious reign—not a stifling rule, but one that is freeing and satisfying.

As we can see in the opening chapters of Genesis, this is not a far-off Creator, but the one who has made us for relationship—a *covenant* relationship—with himself. Unlike a contract, a covenant establishes an ongoing relationship between two parties, and in biblical covenants, the amazing and glorious truth is that the eternal, uncreated God chooses to be our God and to make us his people so that we can have the enormous privilege of knowing, loving, and serving him (Gen. 17:7; Exod. 6:7).

God created Adam and Eve as the first humans, and, in his plan, specifically Adam was formed with the privilege of representing all humans. God gave everything to him. Everything except one thing: the tree of the knowledge of good and evil.

God's command not to eat the fruit from this tree functioned as a test (Gen. 2:15–17). Because God was the Creator and Lord, he had the right to demand perfect obedience from Adam. But would this first man joyfully love and obey God and enjoy the purpose of his creation—namely, to know and love God in fullness of covenant relationship forever? Because God rules as a kind and generous Father, would this cause the one he created to delight in his rule?[3] Or would God's creation reject his rule and come under the sentence of death—the natural consequence of rejecting the one who is life?

You can guess the answer. Sadly, tragically for the human race, suspicious of the Lord's kind and good rule, Adam chooses the latter.

It is crucial to see that this choice Adam made was no mere inadvertent mistake. Instead, it was an act of wilful rebellion against and rejection of the God of all glory, love, holiness, goodness, and life. This is why the human problem is so serious. And

---

3 Reeves, *Delighting in the Trinity*, 24.

it is because of Adam's sin that, even many centuries later, we still need a specific kind of Saviour to undo the damage that he did. Just as Adam's headship defines what it means to be human, his breaking of God's command in Genesis 3 would bring sin and death into the world, affecting all people everywhere (Rom. 3:23). From this point forwards, the communion with God that we were made to enjoy was broken. We have become sinners curved in on ourselves, as we have become lovers of self rather than lovers of God (2 Tim. 3:2–4).

What exactly is wrong with us?

God created us to know and love him, to rule over creation, and to display his glory (Gen. 1:26–30; Ps. 8:4–8). What an awesome privilege and calling—if only it could have stayed that way! But due to Adam's sin, what happened to him, and then by extension to all of us, was truly catastrophic for the whole human race.

Scripture makes for difficult reading at

this point. It pulls no punches.

First, Adam's sin rendered him guilty and corrupted. This had an impact on the entire creation, for, afterwards, the God who had made everything good (Gen. 1:31) placed a curse on creation (Rom. 8:18–25). So, after Adam, we all live in a fallen world that only God can remedy.

Second, Adam's sin was not merely his own, but it was passed on to each one of us. The book of Genesis confirms this; by chapter 6, human sin had so multiplied that it resulted in a disastrous global flood, wiping out the world's population other than Noah and his family.

Looking back on the course of human history, Paul, in the New Testament, also confirms our universal fallenness: "None is righteous, no, not one ... for all have sinned and fall short of the glory of God" (Rom. 3:10, 23). In fact, Adam's sin that we inherit and imitate has brought us under the sentence of death (6:23). We were made to know, love, and serve God, but now we are spiritually dead and therefore live under his judgement as his enemies and objects of his righteous anger (Eph. 2:1–3).

Third, following the sin in the Garden of Eden, God expelled Adam and Eve from his presence (Genesis 3). The only way back into relationship with him from then on would be by God's own provision.

Thankfully, mercifully, this isn't the end of the story. And even in the moments just following Adam's sin, in light of who God is, we see his overflow of love—hope glimmering on the distant horizon. Though God didn't have to save us, there was a glimpse that he would.

This glimpse came in the form of God's promise to provide an "offspring" of Eve who would undo what Adam had done. Speaking to the serpent after Adam and Eve have sinned, God says:

> I will put enmity between you and the woman, and between your offspring and her offspring; he shall bruise your head,

and you shall bruise his heel. (Gen. 3:15)

Remember that God is holy and just, that sin is always against *him,* and sin must be punished. God is not like a human judge, one who adjudicates laws external to himself, but rather, God *is* the law (Ps. 51:4). And so, for God to forgive us, he must remain true to himself—which is a wondrously good thing! Yet it also means that our forgiveness requires the full satisfaction of his moral demand.

So God's promise in Genesis 3 that one who descends from Eve will destroy the serpent's work creates a legitimate question. God must punish our sin, but if he also promises to forgive our sin and undo what Adam did, then how, realistically, could he achieve this? How could God both save and punish?

As the Holy One, God is "the Judge of all the earth" who always does what is right (Gen. 18:25). Given our sin, we can never meet his righteous demand in our own strength—any more than we can pull ourselves up by our own bootstraps. We are alienated from God, guilty and condemned; we are under the sentence of death and powerless to do anything about it.

Who can satisfy God's righteous demand other than God himself? This is *the* major question that drives the Bible's story, and it is a crucial one for us today, because unless we grasp its importance, we won't see why we need a specific Saviour to meet our need and to remedy the problem of our sin.

Salvation must come from God alone (Jonah 2:9).

REFLECT or DISCUSS

1. Why is it so important to understand who God is?
2. What are some common misconceptions about why we were created? Why, according to Scripture, were we created?
3. In light of who God is and why he created us, why is sin so ugly?

3

The Saviour Who Meets Our Need

As we follow the storyline of Scripture after sin enters the world, what we discover is that God gloriously and graciously provides for us. Though our need is great, God's response is greater: a Saviour who meets our need.

Old Testament anticipation

After Adam's sin, God doesn't leave us to ourselves. Thankfully. Instead, he acts with kindness: he promises to reverse the effects of sin by providing an "offspring" of "the woman" (Gen. 3:15)—an enigmatic promise whose implications will become clearer over time. This first "gospel promise" creates the expectation that when it is finally realised, sin and death will be destroyed and God's saving rule will be established on earth. God will provide a Saviour to undo what Adam did and restore goodness to the world.

What glorious news! But who exactly is this "offspring"?

First, the words of Genesis 3:15 indicate that the coming Saviour must be truly human, since he comes from the woman. Because by his perfect obedience he will undo what Adam did, it is important that he must be human like us—and yet he is not like us, for he is a greater Adam (see Rom. 5:14; 1 Cor. 15:45, 47).

This truth is further underscored through successive covenants that God makes over time with Noah, Abraham, Israel, Moses, and David. Each of them picks up the "offspring" promise. But as the Old Testament makes painfully clear, not one of those God makes a covenant with can save us, for they too need a Saviour. Instead, all of them point forward to someone who can do what they can't: the sinless covenant-keeper who will love God perfectly, obeying all God's commands and satisfying God's righteous demand against us.

This truth is especially evident in the covenant of God with David. The Davidic covenant is the epitome of the Old Testament covenants, for it brings the previous ones to a climax in King David himself. The Davidic covenant consists of God's promises about the establishment of David's house forever (2 Sam. 7:12–16) and is notably characterised by the "Father-son" relationship between God and the king (v. 14; Psalm 2). Significantly, this Father-son relationship links the Davidic covenant back to the previous covenants (for example, Adam, Abraham, and Israel) as well as forwards to Jesus, who is David's greater Son.

Previously, the language of "son" was applied to the nation of Israel (Exod. 4:22–23), but now it is applied to the individual king as the representative of that nation. As king, David represents both God's rule to the people and the people themselves as a whole (2 Sam. 7:18–29). The Davidic king also fulfils the role of Adam, since it is through him that God's rule is effected on earth (v. 19). At the centre of God's redemptive plan is the restoration of humanity's role in creation by the provision of a human "offspring." By the time we get to David, God is teaching us that it is specifically through the Davidic king that creation will be restored—a truth strongly emphasised in the Psalms and the writings of the prophets (e.g., Psalm 2, 72, 110; Isa. 9:6–7 and chapter 11).

However, a problem remains. All the Davidic kings disobey, just like Adam did, yet God's promise of a Saviour depends on them. God will surely keep his promise to provide the king who will bring salvation, won't he? But among the kings, there is not even one faithful and obedient son/king who can save us.

What mere human can rise to this level? After all, only God can forgive sin, bring his kingdom to this world, and usher in a new creation. Only a Saviour who is truly God would ever be in a position to achieve this.

This leads us to the message of the biblical prophets, who unveil the second truth: this coming Saviour must also be truly God. How so? The prophets announce that God will keep his promise to save us by his provision of a faithful king who is also a priest (Psalm 110; Isa. 9:6–7). In this human king-priest, a new and everlasting covenant will commence, resulting in God's saving reign in this world, the permanent forgiveness of our sin (Jer. 31:34), and the inauguration of a new creation (Isa. 65:17).

The prophets teach that the future king-priest will be both a human and a divine "Son." Isaiah pictures this well. The future human king will sit on David's throne (Isa. 9:7), but he will also bear the names of God: "Wonderful Counselor, Mighty God, Everlasting Father, Prince of Peace" (v. 6). This king, though another David (Isa. 11:1), is also David's Lord, who shares God's rule (Ps. 110:1). He is the mediator of a new covenant, that is, the one who acts on our behalf, who does not only the acts of God, but also dies in our place for our sin (Isa. 53:11).

It is through him alone that forgiveness comes (Jer. 31:34). In him, Old Testament hope and expectation are now joined: God will save us through his provision of a king/son-priest—one who is truly human and truly God.

New Testament fulfilment

This brings us to a key part of the story: the New Testament fulfilment of what the Old Testament anticipated. Jesus arrives on the scene.

Let's look at Jesus through two lenses, focusing first on his humanity and then on his divinity.

First, Jesus is a *human* son (Matt. 1:1). He fulfils the roles of the previous sons for our salvation, such as Adam (Luke 3:38; Rom. 5:14; Heb. 2:5–18), Abraham (Gal. 3:16), Israel (Exod. 4:22–23; Hosea 11:1; Matt. 2:13–15), and David (2 Sam. 7:14; Psalm 2; 110; Luke 1:69; Rev. 5:5). By his incarnation—that is, by becoming human and living on earth—Jesus ushers in God's kingdom. In Jesus, God's rule and reign has come to this world in bodily form, and in him, God is now making all things right. Furthermore, in his death, Jesus will establish a new covenant, which will result in the complete forgiveness of our sins, just as the Old Testament anticipated.

But there is still more. In his resurrection from the dead, Jesus inaugurates the new creation, demonstrating that sin and death have been defeated. And due to his work as our great Saviour and Lord, Jesus returns to his Father and is now seated on his throne, ruling over all nations and peoples and sovereignly bringing history to its divinely purposed end, or consummation, at his return (Matt. 28:18–20; Acts 2:32–36; Phil. 2:9–11; Heb. 1:1–3).

Second, Jesus is the *divine Son* of the Father (Matt. 11:25–30; John 1:1–18). For, of course, it is only as the eternal "Word [who] became flesh" (John 1:1, 14) that he can fulfil the Law and the Prophets (Matt. 5:17–20; Luke 24:44–49), bear our sin, and establish a new covenant in his blood (Rom. 3:21–26; Eph. 1:7–10; Hebrews 7–10).

That is a lot to take in. But it is worth reflecting on, because all of it shows why Jesus, and Jesus alone, meets our need. He must be *human* to identify with us so that he can obey for us as our covenant representative and undo what Adam did. Yet Jesus must also be the *divine* Son to be our substitute to accomplish the full forgiveness of our sin (Rom. 4:25).

Remember that our greatest problem is our fractured relationship with God. Sin results in many disastrous effects, as we now know, but its greatest consequence is our state of condemnation before God (Rom. 6:23; Eph. 2:1–3). Given who God is, Job's question is a haunting one: "How can a man be in the right before God?" (Job 9:2). Since God cannot overlook our sin, he alone must satisfy his own holy demand against us as God—which is precisely what he has done for us in our perfect Saviour!

But this is where our world takes offense.

Only one person? Really? To say that there is only *one* person who can meet our need sounds too exclusive. Are there not *many* ways to God?

The answer is found in God's Word. There is only *one* Saviour who meets our need because there is only *one* Saviour who is human yet stands in perfect relation to God—because he is God. Scripture unambiguously teaches, "And there is salvation in no one else, for there is no other name under heaven given among men by which we must be saved" (Acts 4:12). There can be no alternate way because there is no substitute for Jesus *himself*.

The Bible's claim that Jesus is the only way isn't a hammer to hit people with or a platform from which to look down on others. And it's not that there really are many ways to God, but Scripture arbitrarily narrows it down to one. Rather, Jesus Christ is the only way because of who he is: he is the only one who can meet our need. The eternal reward of salvation is the promise of being with Jesus himself: "I will come again and will take you to myself" (John 14:3). This is why it doesn't make sense to say that there are other ways to God, for there is no substitute for Jesus himself, and he alone can do what we cannot do.

Once God has opened our eyes to the truth of our helpless condition to save ourselves, we will rejoice in God's provision of this Jesus who alone can meet our need in his perfect life, death, and resurrection for us (Heb. 7:26–27). And since all that Jesus does for us is perfect, complete, and finished, we can't add anything to his work. All that is left for us is to receive him by faith, and to know, love, and worship him now and forever. Hymn writer Philip Bliss captured this message so well many years ago:

Lifted up was he to die;
"It is finished!" was his cry;
Now in heav'n exalted high.
Hallelujah! What a Saviour![1]

1 Philip P. Bliss, "Hallelujah! What a Saviour!" (1875).

We've only begun to scratch the surface of our reflecting on Christ's "finished" work. Let us now turn to unpack some of the richness and fullness of what our Lord Jesus Christ has done for us as our holy and all-sufficient Lord and Saviour.

REFLECT or DISCUSS

1. What, according to Isaiah 9:6, are some of the names of "the future king-priest"? What do these names tell us about him?
2. What are some reasons that God's provision of Jesus as our Saviour should cause a sinner to rejoice?
3. Why does the world find the biblical gospel offensive? How might believers respond to critiques of the claim that Jesus is the only way to salvation?

4

Our True and Final Prophet

"Hallelujah, what a Saviour!" This line from the lyrics of Philip Bliss's hymn are fitting praise for the one who "loved us and gave himself up for us" (Eph. 5:2). My hope is that the more you grasp who Jesus is, the more you'll find yourself rejoicing in him.

But trying to capture all that our Lord Jesus achieved in the fullness of his perfect, complete, and finished work is difficult. In a short book like this, it is even more of a challenge. So, how can we break it down a bit in order to appreciate the richness of who Jesus is and what he's done?

Personally, I've found that one helpful way of meeting this challenge is by reflecting on Christ's work as our great prophet, then as our great priest, and then as our great king.[1] These three roles depict well the finished nature of Christ's work because they connect his earthly work to the Old Testament expectation of a coming Saviour who will be a prophet, priest, and king. As God's plan is unveiled over time, we see why and how Christ fulfils each of these expectations perfectly and thereby meets our every need.

Starting with Adam in the first chapters of Genesis, the Old Testament introduces us to human prophets, priests, and kings. In their various roles, they illuminate specific aspects of our need. Sin has affected our knowledge of God, hence we need a prophet to reveal him to us. Sin has also rendered us guilty before God, hence our need for a priest to atone for our sins. And sin has made us rebels who refuse to submit to God's rule, hence the need for a king to subdue our hearts and

1 Christ's work as our prophet, priest, and king is also called his "threefold office"—a teaching that goes back to the early church but was uniquely developed by John Calvin and the heirs of the Protestant Reformation. See John Calvin, *Institutes of the Christian Religion*, ed. John T. McNeill; trans. Ford Lewis Battles (Philadelphia: Westminster, 1960), 2.15.

bring God's sovereign rule to this world. But, as noted earlier, none of these individuals in their different roles can save us, for ultimately, they too need a perfect Lord and Saviour over them.

Instead, the prophets, priests, and kings who appear in the Old Testament point forward to our Lord Jesus Christ, the one who perfectly fulfils their roles. For in Jesus Christ alone do we see God's resolution to reveal himself to us in truth, to take away our guilt and sin, to satisfy his own righteous requirements, to reverse the horrible effects of the fall, and to make this world right by the establishment or giving of a new covenant in his blood.

Let's dig more deeply into what Jesus Christ has done as prophet, priest, and king. To begin, we'll focus on what Scripture tells us about his prophetic work, considering two questions in turn:

- Why is a prophet necessary?
- Why is Christ the true and final Prophet?

Why is a prophet necessary?

A prophet is one who speaks God's word to the people. But why do we need such a person?

First, we need a prophet because, as finite creatures, we need God to reveal objective truth to us. Although creation indirectly reveals some truths about God (Ps. 19:1–6), this is not enough to enable us to know God himself, nor the specifics of his plan, purposes, and promises. In fact, even before the fall, God had to speak to Adam so that he would know God's command. God never intended for us to know truth apart from divine revelation, first in creation and then, more significantly, by divine speech.

Is this an important point to grasp? Relevant and useful? Absolutely! In fact, it relates directly to a pressing question of our day: whether objective truth is indeed real and possible to know. Our culture is in the midst of a crisis of authority. People have embraced pluralism, which at its heart denies that there is an objective ground for truth. But if this is so, then on what basis do we decide what is true, good, and beautiful?

Pluralistic thinking underlies something further that affects our human relationships: we are repeatedly told that we must accept everyone's personal "truth" as legitimate, and we have no right to question it. After all, for us to question another's "truth" assumes that we have an objective standard to judge it by, which our society flatly denies. For this reason, we are expected to accept all truth, moral, and religious claims as equal, however illogical that may appear in its outworkings. Otherwise, we are accused of wrongly valuing our own views too highly or of forcing our beliefs on someone else.

But reality isn't just whatever you make it to be. God has created an objective world that reflects his plan, and since he is the source and standard of truth, objective truth is not only possible, but a reality. And the way we know truth is through God's own initiative to speak to us. This is why we can know God truly, and also know something about ourselves and the world. We have his divine revelation through the biblical prophets/authors who give us God's written Word. So, the Bible rejects pluralistic thinking outright.

Second, a prophet is necessary because sin renders all humans spiritually blind and bent on distorting the truth and rejecting God's Word (Rom. 1:18–32; 2 Cor. 4:4; Eph. 17–19). Scripture pictures sinful humanity as groping in the dark and yet deliberately suppressing God's clear and authoritative revelation. In our sinful state, we readily believe lies because we refuse to fear God in our thinking, rejecting his standard of truth (Ps. 14:1; Prov. 1:7). As limited and now fallen humans, we cannot "live by bread alone, but by every word that comes from the mouth of God" (Matt. 4:4).

Again, this is a crucial point to grasp, and to rejoice in. God has not left us to figure out things on our own, apart from his Word. Through his appointed prophets, God has given us Scripture for us to know him—his nature, character, promises, and plan—and to correct our distortion of the truth. How thankful we ought to be for God's prophetic word, but even more, that our Lord Jesus brings God's prophetic word to fulfilment and completion!

Why is Christ the true and final Prophet?

If we truly need a prophet, couldn't God have chosen anyone to speak for him? What makes Jesus Christ the true and final Prophet who brings the word of the Old Testament prophets to finality and completeness?

This is best seen by comparing Christ to Moses. Among God's people, Moses was regarded as the key prophet, indeed, the paradigm of Old Testament prophets, and for good reason. God spoke "face to face" with Moses (Num. 12:6–8). Moses was the author of the first five books of the Bible (or "Pentateuch"). And God promised that after Moses died, he would raise up a prophet like him (Deut. 18:15–19). In this way, Moses became the pattern for all the prophets who followed, anticipating the true and final prophet to come.

As we now know, that true and final prophet is Jesus, who is greater than Moses and all the prophets who preceded him. Jesus not only speaks God's word, as the other prophets did, but he *is* the divine Word. Thus, he is the source and standard of divine revelation (John 1:1). All the other prophets spoke under God's authority using these words: "Thus says the Lord." But Jesus says, "I say to you…" (Matt. 5:22). Jesus, the eternal Word, speaks on his own authority as the one who perfectly reveals the Father since he is one with the Father (John 1:1; 10:30).

Is it any wonder that Jesus can say, "I am the way, and *the truth,* and the life" (John 14:6; emphasis added)? Or that John can say, "No one has ever seen God; the only God, who is at the Father's side, he has made him known" (1:18)? Although some saw visions of God in the Old Testament (Exodus 33–34; Isa. 6:5), nobody saw God himself directly before the divine Son became human. But now, in Christ, we have seen God, and we have heard God's direct Word through him. This is why

Jesus is the true and final Prophet. And his prophetic ministry is in a different category from all the others, including Moses'.

Hebrews 1:1–3 teaches us this too. The author of Hebrews demonstrates Christ's prophetic superiority in light of Christ's status as the divine Son. In him, the creator and sustainer of the universe (vv. 2–3), the "radiance" of God's glory, and the "exact imprint of [God's] nature" (v. 3), God has spoken finally, definitively, and completely. Yes, previous prophetic revelation was authoritative, but it was incomplete, and it anticipated what was to come "by his Son" (v. 2). All of God's revelation has now been fulfilled and perfected in Christ.

Jesus Christ was a prophet during his earthly ministry, but his prophetic work extends far beyond those brief years. It persists throughout Scripture, both in the Old and the New Testament. Prior to the incarnation, God's revelation was mediated through the Son and by the Spirit to the prophets (1 Pet. 1:1–12), which gave us our

Old Testament. After Christ's ascension and return back to the Father's right hand to rule and to reign (Acts 1:1–9; Rom. 8:34; Eph. 1:20–22), God's revelation is mediated through the Son and by the Spirit to the apostles (John 16:5–15; Acts 2:42), which gives us our New Testament. So, by speaking through the prophets and the apostles, our Lord spoke to us both before his coming to live among us and after his departure.

There is never a time in human history when Christ doesn't speak to his people with complete authority. Although the Old Testament revelation reaches its fulfilment in Christ, as recorded in the Gospels, *all* of Scripture is actually Christ's Word, which means that we are never without the Word of our great, final, and glorious Prophet. God certainly wants us to know him in truth!

All of this is good news for you and for me. Christ's Word that was given to us in Scripture is enough to bring us the instruction we need not only for our salvation, but also for our entire lives. Because of who Jesus is, and because Scripture is his Word, it is not only trustworthy, but it is all we need in order to know God, to know ourselves, to grow in our Christian lives, and to walk in ways that are pleasing to him. Instead of having to fumble around in the dark, we find that God's Word is "a lamp to [our] feet and a light to [our] path" (Ps. 119:105). This is why Scripture alone has to be our *final* authority in matters of truth and salvation, and why it must govern every single aspect of our lives.

Applying Christ's prophetic work

Paul's words of exhortation to the Colossian church connect Christ's prophetic work with the ins and outs of our day-to-day lives.

In his letter to the Colossians, Paul expresses concern that the church members are building their lives on a combination of the world's thought and Christ. This doesn't work: in the end, it leads to a syncretism that denies Christ. Instead, he tells them not to build their lives on "philosophy and empty deceit, according to human tradition," but to build their lives "according to Christ." Why? For this profound reason: "In [Christ] the whole fullness of deity dwells bodily" (Col. 2:8–9). In other words, in Christ is found all truth, knowledge, and wisdom. Human tradition, if not grounded in Christ, becomes merely relative, which ultimately leads to disaster.

This is why Paul exhorts us to build our lives on the source and standard of truth, and to do so by obedience to Christ and his entire revelation given in Scripture. Yes, God has spoken to us in creation, and we can learn from it. But it is in his special, written revelation—namely, the Bible, which reveals to us our incomparable Lord Jesus—that he has given us everything we need for saving knowledge and growth in our Christian lives (see 2 Pet. 1:3). This gift of God's Word is an outworking of the prophetic ministry of Jesus.

What is your response? Our response to Christ and his Word should be that of Peter when Jesus asked his disciples, "Do you want to go away as well?" Peter answered, "Lord, to whom shall we go? You have the words of eternal life" (John 6:67–68). Our temptation today, as it was for the Colossians, is to listen to the ideas of the world. But to avoid being "tossed to and fro by the waves and carried about by every wind of doctrine" (Eph. 4:14), we must gladly and joyfully submit our lives to our Lord Jesus, and "take every thought captive to obey Christ" (2 Cor. 10:5), who is our true and final Prophet.

There can be no better way.

REFLECT or DISCUSS

1. Why do we need a prophet? A priest? A king?
2. Why can Christ be described as our "true and final Prophet"?
3. How would you explain that "Jesus is the only way" to a friend or relative who has embraced pluralism?
4. What did Paul tell the Colossian church, and why? What does this mean for us today?

5

Our Great High Priest

As crucial as Christ's great prophetic work is, we need more than a teacher of truth, for our human problem is more than ignorance. We also stand guilty before God. As such, we need someone to represent us, to pay for our sin, to cleanse us from our defilement, and to reconcile us to our holy God. In other words, what we desperately need is a priest.

Unless we are familiar with the Bible, such language probably sounds foreign. Today, the word "priest" may conjure up ideas of Wiccans or obscure religious practices. Or you might think of formal robes and ceremonies. This is likely far removed from anything you experience in everyday life. However, in Scripture, we discover that a worthy priest is essential to our salvation. In fact, we won't understand the meaning of Jesus' cry, "It is finished," without grasping that he achieved our salvation as our "great high priest."

Let's explore this further using three questions as our guide:

- What is a priest?
- Why do we need a priest?
- Why is the Lord Jesus Christ the *great* high priest who perfectly meets our need?

What is a priest?

Broadly speaking, a priest is a person who fulfils a religious function by standing between God and humans. Thus, the job of a priest is to act as a "mediator." In our daily lives, we are familiar with mediators such as lawyers who represent us before judges or ambassadors who are go-betweens on behalf of nations. In Scripture, however, the primary role of the mediator was to bring two parties together—namely, God and humans. Hebrews 5:1

captures this truth well: "Every high priest chosen from among men is appointed to act on behalf of men in relation to God, to offer gifts and sacrifices for sins."

In Scripture, the "high priest" holds the top rank among priests and officiates the most solemn and sacred ceremonies, and in Israel, the office of high priest was reserved for Aaron and his direct descendants—those from the tribe of Levi (Exod. 29:9, 44; Num. 3:10; 18:1–7). God chose the Levites to represent his people as go-betweens standing between them and himself, a crucial job indeed! The idea is that apart from the work of the priests, the people of Israel—and by extension all of us—remain separated from God, unable to come into his presence, and oblivious to the purpose of our creation: to be in covenant relationship with him.

Why do we need a priest?

In the New Testament, Hebrews 5:1 summarises the primary job of the high priest as follows: "To offer gifts and sacrifices for sins." Standing as a mediator between sinful people and a holy God, the high priest offered sacrifices that covered the people's sin and satisfied God's judicial anger against it.

Most fundamentally, we need such a priest because, as we've seen, we have disobeyed God, rebelling against him, and as such, in our sin we are alienated from God and under the sentence of death (Rom. 3:23; 6:23; Eph. 2:1–3). We need someone to act on our behalf so that we can be declared just before God and experience his covenantal presence once again. Unless this takes place, there is no hope for us. A priest is vitally important—it's a matter of life and death!

Yet Scripture is clear: we don't need just any priest; we need a perfect one—indeed, one who is truly human so that he can actually represent us by obeying God perfectly, and one who is truly God in order to be our substitute and satisfy God's righteous demands against us.

Only one person fits this description: Jesus.

Why is Jesus the *great* high priest who meets our need?

Just as there are many prophets mentioned in Scripture, so too there are many priests. In God's plan, he intended other human prophets and priests to meet our need, at least in a provisional way, but also to point forward to Christ, revealing why he alone brings a permanent, complete, and final salvation.

The high priests of the Old Testament operated under the Mosaic covenant. They carried out their religious duties daily, and their work brought about only a relative and temporary forgiveness. In God's plan, he never intended for their work—specifically, their offering of animal sacrifices for the people on a daily and yearly basis—to be an end in itself. Rather, God designed the sacrificial system to reveal the need for a greater priest, a greater sacrifice, and indeed, a greater covenant (Psalm 110; Jer. 31:31–34): the one Jesus established by his death on the cross (Hebrews 8).

The book of Hebrews is an excellent place to begin when thinking about the contrasts between Christ and the priests of the tribe of Levi ("Levitical priests"). Such priests were fallen people who need a Saviour themselves. In truth, they could not adequately represent us (Heb. 5:2–3; 9:7). But Christ, the divine, sinless Son, took on our humanity so that he can perfectly represent us in his person and his resurrection (7:23–24). This is why he "is able to save to the uttermost those who draw near to God through him" (7:25). Levitical priests offered the blood of bulls and goats as sacrifices that mediated a temporary forgiveness, but this could never pay permanently for their and the people's sins (8:3; 10:1–4). Christ offered himself as the perfect sacrifice and substitute that paid completely for our sins (7:25–27; 9:12; 10:15–18), thereby securing our eternal redemption (9:11–15).

The proof that Jesus' high priestly work was far greater than the work of the Levitical priests was that by his death he established a new and better covenant (Hebrews 8). Remember that the promise of the new covenant is that God will grant a *full and permanent forgiveness of sin* (Jer. 31:34; Heb. 10:15–18), something that the Levitical priests under the sacrificial system of the Mosaic covenant never could achieve. Due to Christ's death on the cross, we now have permanent forgiveness of sin, which was why Jesus could cry out, "It is finished!" Christ has finished his priestly work and paid for our sin in full—the greatest news imaginable!

For the believer, this means that there is nothing we can add. Jesus has borne all our sin and thus has secured our justification before God, our reconciliation with him, and our redemption. In Christ alone, we have a full, effective, and complete salvation, unlike the "shadow" of the old covenant (see Col. 2:17). We have a high priest who meets our every need—our all-sufficient Redeemer and exalted Lord (Heb. 7:25–28).

But the flipside is also true: apart from Christ, there can be no salvation.

Christ alone

Christ alone is our "wisdom from God, righteousness and sanctification and redemption" (1 Cor. 1:30). By his obedient life and death, "he has perfected for all time those who are being sanctified" (Heb. 10:14).

But sadly, in our sin, we foolishly continue to think that we have something to contribute. We're like a child who brings his pennies to a parent to help buy an expensive house, thinking that it's enough when it's totally insignificant.

This attitude can spring up in at least two ways.

On the one hand, in Roman Catholic thought, although the exclusivity of Christ is affirmed, the sufficiency of Christ's work is undercut. Christ isn't viewed as the sole ground of our justification, received by faith alone apart from works. Instead, Rome claims that Christ paid for our past/original sin but not our present and future sins. We are forgiven of the latter by receiving grace through the sacraments dispensed by the church: as we are infused with grace, our nature is transformed, and we are able to cooperate with God to merit eternal life. Thus, we are saved by a combination of Christ's merit *and* our sacramental incorporation into Christ through the church.

But Scripture teaches clearly that we are justified solely by Christ and by *his* merits, not a combination of what Christ has done and our grace-empowered cooperation. In Christ's obedient life and death for us, God's righteous demand has already been met; Christ's righteousness is now imputed—that is, legally reckoned to us as believers—because of his covenant representation and substitution; and the Holy Spirit who raises us spiritually from the dead unites us to Christ so that his work is now applied to us (Eph. 2:4–10). There is not one thing we can add (Gal. 3:10–14; Heb. 2:17–18; 5:1–10; 7:23–28; 9:15–28). Christ achieved the full satisfaction and payment of our sin, which includes our past, present, and future sins. And by faith-union in Christ, we stand complete, justified before God and clothed in *his* righteousness (Rom. 4:1–8; 5:1–2).

On the other hand, evangelicals can also get things wrong and think that they contribute to Christ's work. They may believe that to be a "good Christian," we must act a certain way. This is not necessarily wrong, for we seek to obey God's Word in our lives every day. But if we are not careful, we can think that by "doing" specific things, we are acceptable and pleasing to God.

Works are the fruit of saving faith, but they do not contribute to our justification. We are not to rest in our good works, sincere love, or even our "faith," apart from faith *in Christ*. As Herman Bavinck rightly reminded us,

> The righteousness which justifies us, therefore, is not to be separated from the person of Christ. … There is no possibility of sharing in the benefits of Christ without being in fellowship with the person of Christ. … In order to stand before the judgment of God, to be acquitted of all

> guilt and punishment, and to share in the glory of God and eternal life, we must have Christ, not something of Him, but Christ Himself.[1]

The life of the Christian is not a life of religious performance in the hopes of one day earning God's favour. The one who is in Christ is continually forgiven, loved, and welcomed into the life of the Trinity. Christ lives to intercede for us and holds us close to the Father even in our weaknesses (Heb. 7:25). Our salvation does not rest on our merit, but on his.

With the perfect Son of God as our great high priest, we have a secure place to rest. Even when we are discouraged by our continued sin and failure to overcome it, he is faithful to love and care for us. Christ's mediation between God and humans is fully sufficient to cover every sin. What's more, he stands in heaven with

1 Herman Bavinck, *The Wonderful Works of God*, trans. Henry Zylstra (repr., Philadelphia: Westminster Seminary Press, 2019), 436.

compassion in his heart as he prays for us continually, preserving our faith as our high priest and Redeemer.

REFLECT or DISCUSS

1. What do you think of, or imagine in your mind's eye, when you hear the word "priest"? How would you describe what a priest does in your own words?
2. How does the writer of Hebrews 5:1 describe the role of a priest?
3. How does Christ as priest meet us in our need? What is his heart towards sinners?

6
Our Sovereign King

If people have heard anything about Jesus, they often identify him as a Saviour. After all, didn't the angels announce to the shepherds at Jesus' birth, "For unto you is born this day in the city of David a Savior, who is Christ the Lord" (Luke 2:11)? But what is often forgotten is that the angels, along with the entire New Testament, also proclaimed that Jesus is the Lord of all and Lord over all.

This is vital. Many outside the church wrongly view Jesus simply as a nice man or an interesting leader, someone we might look up to or admire. Too many inside the church view him as a tamer version of C. S. Lewis' lion, Aslan. No doubt, Jesus *is* kind and gentle, but he is a kind and gentle sovereign King and Judge of the universe. He is our Saviour *and* our Lord. Without properly acknowledging him as the King, we will fail to know him for who he truly is and never grasp why he alone deserves all of our trust, love, and obedient devotion.

With this in view, let's reflect on Christ as our sovereign King by considering the answer to three questions:

- Why a king?
- Why do we need a king?
- Why is Christ *the* King and Lord over all?

Why a king?

In Scripture, there are two complementary ways of thinking about Christ as Lord and King. First, Christ is Lord because of who he is as God the Son. As the divine Son, along with the Father and Spirit, he is the Creator, Lord, and sovereign ruler of all things (Col. 1:15–17; Heb. 1:3). But second, Christ is Lord and King because of what he does for us in his saving work. This latter way of thinking of Christ's lordship will be our primary focus here.

This second sense emphasises Christ's work for us as the eternal Son who became human to undo what Adam did and to save us from our sin. Remember: Adam and Eve were the first royal couple, and by extension, all of us are kings and queens; as God's image-bearers, we were created to rule over the world (Gen. 1:26–31; Psalm 8). But after the fall, although we still continue to bear the divine image, it is now distorted and defaced (Gen. 9:6), requiring our Lord Jesus to come to reconcile us to God and to restore us to the purpose of our creation. In this way, Christ, who is eternally King, becomes King in time by becoming human, obeying for us in his life, dying as our substitute, being raised from the dead to ascend to God's right hand, and now ruling over the entire universe as the King of kings and Lord of lords.

Why do we need a king?

Sin not only renders us guilty before God; it

also enslaves us. Paul captures the horrible effects of sin both by noting our spiritual deadness *and* by stating that we are enslaved to the powers of the world, the flesh, and Satan himself (Eph. 2:1–3; Heb. 2:14–16). Let's face it, we don't like to hear this. We all prefer to think that we are "free" and enslaved to no one. "No one rules over me; I determine my own destiny," we defiantly say. Even a toddler can find her own way of expressing this.

But God's Word disagrees. The power of sin controls our thinking, affections, and desires. We are not "free thinkers," untethered from others' influence, but are enslaved to the mindset of a world that so often controls us. And behind this mindset is the work and activity of Satan, who seeks to ravage and destroy us. We are like Théoden of Rohan from *The Lord of the Rings,* who thinks he is making decisions on his own, but all the while he is simply following the evil thoughts whispered in his ear by Gríma Wormtongue. Also, instead of properly ruling over the earth as God's image-bearers, we eventually discover that the earth puts us "six feet under" as we go to our graves in death.

What we urgently need is a victor to defeat and destroy our enemies—sin, death, and Satan—and to restore us to the purpose of our creation. Apart from such a king, we have no hope. Our only hope can be found in *the* true King, our Lord Jesus Christ. He alone can save us from corruption, defilement, and our utterly helpless condition.

Let's consider this in more depth.

Why is Christ *the* King and Lord over all?

The answer to the question above is the same as for the prophet and priest: it is because of who Jesus is and what he does for us in his saving work. He is above and over all.

In particular, we gain a better idea of why Christ is *the* King when we focus on what he did for us in his resurrection, his ascension, and at Pentecost, when those who were gathered "were all filled with the Holy Spirit" (Acts 2:4). Although we must exercise caution in dividing up Christ's work into specific events since his work is unified, it is helpful to distinguish our Lord's state of humiliation (incarnation, life on earth, and death on a cross) from his state of exaltation (resurrection from the dead, ascension to heaven, and Pentecost). We can more closely identify the former with his priestly work and the latter with his kingly work, although ultimately both roles are necessary for Christ to accomplish our salvation.

With that caveat in mind, let's now see why Christ is *the* King whose work is finished, complete, and perfect as we focus on the three earth-shaking events that make up his state of exaltation.

The resurrection

As Paul reminds us, "For I delivered to you as of first importance what I also received: that Christ died for our sins in accordance with the Scriptures, that he was buried, that he was raised on the third day in accordance with the Scriptures" (1 Cor. 15:3–4). He further explains that "if Christ has not been raised, your faith is futile and you are still in your sins" (v. 17). So, the bodily resurrection of Christ is absolutely central to Christ's saving work.

But why? After all, the Bible knows of other resurrections, such as those of Jarius' daughter and of Lazarus (see Mark 5:21–43; John 11:38–44). What, then, makes Jesus' resurrection so significant?

The difference is found in the one whose resurrection it is and what it signifies. In Scripture, Christ's resurrection is viewed not only as an historical fact (which it is), but also as *the* resurrection of *all* resurrections.

Just think for a moment of all that Christ's resurrection signifies.

First, it signifies that *Christ's work to save his people from their sins is finished*. In paying for our sin, Christ destroyed the power of death. Death had no power over him; rather, he is the conqueror of sin and death (1 Cor. 15:55–57; Col. 2:13–15; Heb. 2:5–18).

Second, Christ's resurrection reveals that *the new creation is here* (1 Cor. 15:20–28;

2 Cor. 5:17). Although we still await *our* resurrection, Christ's resurrection body is the dawning of the new creation and the pattern of what we shall one day be (1 Cor. 15:42–44).

Third, Christ's resurrection guarantees that *what he achieved for us is now also ours,* in faith-union with him. For example, Christ's resurrection ensures our regeneration by the Spirit (Romans 6; Eph. 1:19–20; 1 Pet. 1:3). It is also the ground of our justification (Rom. 4:25; Eph. 2:6), and it guarantees our future glorification as we are conformed to Christ and "patterned" after his glorified human nature (1 Cor. 15:12–58; 2 Cor. 4:14).

Fourth, Christ's resurrection confirms that *God's future judgement is sure.* Paul stresses this truth to the Athenians as he calls and urges them to faith and repentance in Christ (Acts 17:31). In his first coming, Christ comes to destroy sin, death, and Satan, but in his return, he will execute justice. God can't let sin go unpunished forever, and he has given proof of this in Christ's resurrection.

The bottom line is this: Christ's resurrection is central to his work as our victorious King, Judge, and Saviour. It reveals the glorious truths that his work is finished and that even now he is at the Father's right hand, invested with all authority over the entire cosmos (Phil. 2:9–11; Col. 1:15–20). This is nicely captured by the memorable words of Abraham Kuyper: "There is not a square inch in the whole domain of our human existence over which Christ, who is Sovereign over all, does not cry: 'Mine!'"[1]

The ascension and Pentecost

The ascension and Pentecost are often neglected in our thinking about Christ's kingly work. Yet Christ's work is incomplete without these singular events, and both of them also demonstrate why Christ is *the* King and Lord over all.

Christ's ascension is described in Acts 1:6–11 and alluded to in many other places

1 Abraham Kuyper, "Sphere Sovereignty," in *A Centennial Reader*, ed. James D. Bratt (Grand Rapids: Eerdmans, 1998), 488.

in the New Testament (e.g. Luke 24:50–53; Eph. 1:20; Phil. 2:9–11; Heb. 1:3). The fact of the ascension is connected to a number of other truths: Christ has personally departed; he is now seated at the Father's right hand; he is presently ruling over the world (Matt. 28:18; Eph. 1:20–22); and in the future, he will return visibly and publicly (Matt. 24:29–31; Acts 1:11).

Furthermore, given Christ's ascension, we have the confidence that our Lord is accessible to all who call on him (Heb. 4:14) as he continues to intercede for us as our Saviour (Rom. 8:34; Heb. 7:25).

What glorious, reassuring, and encouraging news it is that our sovereign King can help us anywhere in the world (Heb. 4:16; 7:25) as he equips the church for works of service (Eph. 4:8–12)!

Pentecost, the coming of the Holy Spirit, is another key event demonstrating that Christ is King. Why? Because it shows that the long-awaited new-covenant age has arrived. The Old Testament prophets predicted that when

David's greater Son arrived, not only would he have the Spirit in full measure (Isa. 11:1–5; 42:1-8; 61:1–3; Luke 4:17–21), but he would pour out the Holy Spirit on his people, thereby signifying the dawning of the new creation (Ezek. 36:25–27; Joel 2:28–32; Acts 2).

For us, this means that Christ's work is finished; nothing more needs to be added to it. All that is required is for Christ to return and to finish what he inaugurated. Pentecost, as a unique event, is a public demonstration of this wonderful truth. It isn't, then, peripheral to Christ's work, but central to it, since it is the culmination of Christ's ministry on earth.

Thus, by Christ's finished work, he has secured the Spirit for us, already making us share in the new creation even while we await Christ's return. Presently, the Spirit, as the "seal" of God's ownership of us (2 Cor. 1:22; Eph. 1:13; 4:30), testifies that we are God's children, although we await our full rights as "sons" (Rom. 8:14–27; Gal. 4:4–5). Even now, the Spirit is the "firstfruits" of the full harvest (Rom. 8:23; 1 Cor. 15:20, 23), the seal and guarantee of our inheritance (2 Cor. 1:22; 5:5; Eph. 1:14). In fact, the Spirit assures us that our bodies will be raised and thus that we will share in the glorious existence of the final, consummated state (1 Cor. 15:42–44).

In all these ways, the giving of the Spirit at Pentecost signifies the finality, perfection, and finished nature of Christ's work for us.

Rest and rejoice

What a Saviour Christ is—a prophet, priest, and king! In his teaching and his Word, he reveals himself to us. In his birth, he is the divine Son who chose to become our mediator, a choice rooted in God's eternal plan. In his life, he is the sovereign priest-king who willingly chose to die for us as our representative and substitute.

In Jesus' death, he paid for our sin, justified us before God, destroyed death, and defeated Satan. In his resurrection, the Father, by the Spirit, exalted him, thus inaugurating the new creation and the promised new-covenant age. From his seat of authority, the exalted Son from the Father pours out the Spirit, demonstrating that he is both Lord and Messiah. And even now, from his heavenly throne, our exalted king-priest rules over his people, governs history, and will return in power to consummate all that he began in his first coming.

Truly, in Christ alone all our needs are met, perfectly and completely. With Christ as our king, we can rest, knowing that nothing occurs in this world apart from his sovereign hand. As Romans 8 reminds us, nothing can separate us from the love of God in Christ Jesus our Lord (vv. 31–39). Not one thing in all of creation.

Due to Christ's work for us, the Father has exalted his incarnate Son to give him "all authority in heaven and on earth" (Matt. 28:18), "to unite all things in him" (Eph. 1:10), to "put all things under his feet," and to make him "head over all things to the church" (v. 22). In Christ, we have a supreme King who does not reign through force or oppression, but through self-giving love, service, and sacrifice. He holds us in his hands and has sealed us with his Spirit, making us his own. His banner over us is love, and he declares before all the world: "You are mine!"

There is nothing more glorious and wonderful than to meditate on, wholeheartedly believe in, and rest in the finished work of our Lord Jesus Christ. May Jesus become more precious to us as we rejoice in him as the One who meets our every need so perfectly and completely. May we sing with the angels in heaven who surround the throne,

> Worthy is the Lamb who was slain,
> to receive power and wealth and wisdom
>   and might
> and honor and glory and blessing! (Rev. 5:12)

REFLECT or DISCUSS

1. Why are Christ's ascension and the pouring out of his Spirit at Pentecost good news for the believer? How does each help us appreciate specific aspects of what Christ has done?
2. How does recognising Jesus as King transform the way we understand true authority and power? How might this contrast with worldly authority?
3. How does Jesus' kingship deepen our understanding of God as a loving, relational being within the Trinity? How does Jesus' kingship bring us joy rather than burden?

7

The Cross: Full Forgiveness Accomplished

Can you now see that, despite the horror of crucifixion, Jesus' cry from the cross, "It is finished," is the best news imaginable?

Jesus' death was no accident of history, nor was it the tragic end of a great man; rather, it was part of God's eternal plan to rescue us from our sin (Heb. 10:5–7; Rev. 13:8). In that plan, the divine Son, in relation to the Father and the Spirit, was appointed to be the mediator of God's people. Our Lord gladly accepted that appointment, with all of its demands and promises. Thus, Christ's incarnation, life, death, resurrection, ascension, and Pentecost aren't events that "just happened" to occur but were perfectly planned from eternity and executed in time as we know it.

So, Jesus' "It is finished" is a cause for great rejoicing: it signifies that Christ has triumphed, has completed what he came to do. He has accomplished *everything* we need for our salvation, everything required so that he can take the church to himself as his rescued bride.

So far, we have focused on Christ's finished work by seeing how he is our true, final, and great prophet, priest, and king. Yet we haven't reflected directly on the cross itself, the very place from which Christ's cry rings out.

Some of us may want to look away from the cross with all its suffering and pain, perhaps emphasising instead God's incarnation, his being "with us" in our humanity (Matt. 1:23). But Bethlehem is not enough; we also need Calvary, for apart from Christ's cross, there can be no reconciliation or justification before God. And Scripture itself often stresses the necessity of Christ's sacrificial death for our sins (v. 21; 1 Cor. 15:3–4). For this reason, we will continue to treasure Christ's all-sufficient work by focusing on the achievement of the cross and what Jesus did there—*for us*.

The glory of the cross

Glory may not be the first thing we think of when contemplating death on a cross. But God's Word presents the glory of Christ's cross as rich and multifaceted, like a precious gemstone that shines forth from many angles and in many directions. All are necessary to appreciate its beauty.

For example, Scripture views the cross as a propitiatory sacrifice—that is, one that satisfies God's holy wrath against us (Rom. 3:24–26; 1 John 2:2; 4:10). Jesus' death on the cross is an act of reconciliation that removes the enmity between God and ourselves so that we have access to God (2 Cor. 5:18–21; Eph. 2:11–22; Col. 1:19–20), and it is an act of redemption by which we are bought back from our enslavement to sin, death, and Satan (Eph. 1:7; Col. 2:13–15; Heb. 2:14–15). But there is even more: the cross is also where Christ's perfect obedience and full payment for sin entirely satisfy God's righteousness and justice (Rom. 3:25–26; 5:9; 2 Cor. 5:21).

None of these descriptions on its own fully captures what our Lord achieved on the cross, but all of them *together* help us to grasp why Christ's work is finished and complete, as well as why he alone perfectly meets our need and does for us what we could never do for ourselves. Indeed, grasping the glory of the cross by unpacking each of its rich aspects would require much more than is written in this book. Even in eternity we will probably never fully fathom all that our Lord did for us. Forever, we will gaze on our Saviour and be lost in wonder, love, and praise.

The beauty of the cross in all of its dimensions is endless. But at its core, Scripture teaches us that the cross is about Jesus Christ standing in our place to deliver us from the punishment for sin that we deserve. Theologians refer to this as *penal substitution*. This wonderful truth about all our Saviour has done helps us understand not only why the divine Son had to die and why he alone can save us; it also helps us grasp in a greater way the profound glory of Christ's finished work.

The cross as penal substitution

It may seem like a mouthful to speak of the cross as a penal substitutionary work, but bear with me, because doing so is vital and is true to the testimony of Scripture. Let's unpack this teaching by considering these two words in turn: *penal* and *substitution*.

Penal has to do with punishment—perhaps you have heard the term *penal colony*, which is a place of exile or imprisonment. We noted earlier that our sin has placed all of us under God's judgement and the penalty of death (Rom. 3:23; 6:23), so, unless someone intervenes, we will reap the punishment our sin has sown.

Substitution refers to the reality that our Lord Jesus died in our place (1 Pet. 3:18). The Bible sometimes speaks of God choosing to rescue and redeem his people instead of leaving us in our sin and under divine judgement. As our new-covenant head, our Lord Jesus Christ became our representative as the greater Adam, willingly obeying the Father perfectly for us (Rom. 5:12–21). On the cross, Christ took our place and paid our debt by receiving the penalty we deserved (Rom. 3:24–26; Gal. 3:13). The result of his work is that by faith-union in Christ, God the Father declares us just, forgiven of every sin (Rom. 8:1, 32; 2 Cor. 5:21), and free from sin's power and the tyranny of Satan, who once held the verdict of death and condemnation over our heads (Col. 2:13–15; Heb. 2:14–16).

Thus, penal substitution is simply the proclamation of the gospel of God's sovereign grace. It is not just a technical term that pertains to the cross; it is shorthand for speaking of the triune God in all his holiness, justice, wisdom, compassion, and love. It rightly conveys the truth that all of us stand guilty before God, depraved and helpless. It also reminds us of our glorious Saviour—the Substitute—whose cross-work accomplished everything for us. In our place, he bears the penalty we deserve, and by doing so, he saves us completely.

Most significantly, penal substitution places God at the centre of our salvation. It reminds us that the triune God of grace planned our redemption from eternity and then achieved it on the stage of human history, acting in grace to provide and accomplish our salvation by the Father's initiative in and through the Son, and by the Spirit.

"No condemnation now I dread"

I could say so much more about the glory of the cross. Because of Jesus' cross, when we receive him by faith alone, we are justified, reconciled, and redeemed; adopted into God's family; and restored to the purpose of our creation.

In Jesus, we are condemned no more. And the cross isn't just about opening the door to salvation; it's about providing what we need day by day to *grow* in Christ. The cross reveals at the same time the depth of our sin and the reach of God's grace, which is essential for transforming believers' hearts and lives.

Whenever we feel the weight and ugliness of our sin, our coldness of heart, our lack of assurance, that is the time to turn to the cross. There, Christ has already dealt fully and finally with our sin. There we see the full extent of his love. At the cross, strivings cease, the weight of sin is lifted, holiness becomes beautiful, and our hearts are free to adore our one and only Saviour.

The prolific English hymn writer Charles Wesley captures the truth of what Jesus has done for us, and why our salvation in him is truly finished, in these uplifting lyrics that we too can sing:

> No condemnation now I dread;
> Jesus, and all in him, is mine!
> Alive in him, my living Head,
> And clothed in righteousness divine,
> Bold, I approach the eternal throne,
> And claim the crown, through Christ my own.[1]

---

1 Charles Wesley, "And Can It Be" (1738).

REFLECT or DISCUSS

1. "Bethlehem is not enough; we also need Calvary." Why?
2. How would you explain penal substitution in your own words? How does this teaching about the cross deepen our understanding of God's love and justice working together in perfect harmony?
3. What does it mean for your daily life to know that Jesus willingly took the penalty for your sin on the cross? How does this affect your sense of assurance, identity, and relationship with God?

8

No Other Fountain

The Reformer John Calvin (1509–1564) reflected deeply on Christ's finished work and how it affects our Christian lives. He correctly reasoned from Scripture that since our entire salvation is found in Christ alone, then *he* is all that we need.

Calvin paints a beautiful portrait of Christ's sufficiency and calls us to drink deeply of him:

> If we seek salvation, we are taught by the very name of Jesus that it is "of him" [1 Cor. 1:30]. . . . If we seek strength, it lies in his dominion; if purity, in his conception; if gentleness, it appears in his birth. . . . If we seek redemption, it lies in his passion; if acquittal, in his condemnation; if remission

> of the curse, in his cross [Gal. 3:13]; if satisfaction, in his sacrifice; if purification, in his blood; if reconciliation, in his descent into hell; if mortification of the flesh, in his tomb; if newness of life, in his resurrection; if immortality, in the same; if inheritance of the Heavenly Kingdom, in his entrance into heaven; if protection, if security, if abundant supply of all blessings, in his Kingdom; if untroubled expectation of judgment, in the power given to him to judge. In short, since rich store of every kind of good abounds in him, let us drink our fill from this fountain, and from no other.[1]

Here, Calvin vividly captures what—no, *who*—is absolutely central to the Christian faith and to our Christian lives: Christ alone.

All that our triune God has done for us is found in Christ. This isn't to diminish the persons of the Father and Holy Spirit, who, together with Christ, are the triune God. But Scripture teaches us that all the Father does

1 Calvin, *Institutes* 2.16.19.

centres in his Son and that the Spirit works to bear witness and bring glory to the Son (John 15:26; 16:13–15). Michael Reeves has wisely reminded us that "the centre, the cornerstone, the jewel in the crown of Christianity is not an idea, a system or a thing; it is not even 'the gospel' as such. It is Jesus Christ."[2] Jesus is the beloved Son of the Father, who has been given a work to do that we couldn't do. By grace, we find our salvation, life, and the very purpose of our existence in knowing him and being rightly related to him.

What does this mean for us today?

First, it requires that we confess, defend, and proclaim the truth of who Jesus is as the exclusive Lord and perfect Saviour. This is a challenge for some of us who live in a secular, pluralistic context that attempts to relativise all truth claims or deny the existence of God. Others of us may live in parts of the world that embrace another religion instead of Christianity. But no matter where we

2 Michael Reeves, *Rejoicing in Christ* (Downers Grove, IL: IVP Academic, 2015), 10.

find ourselves, contrary to the mindset of the world, we must be convinced that Jesus isn't just another religious leader, but the sovereign Lord of the universe who deserves and demands all of our trust, love, devotion, obedience, and service. We must proclaim with vigour, courage, and deep conviction that apart from faith alone in Christ alone, there is no salvation (Acts 4:12).

Second, we must confess the glory of Christ and his finished work not only with our words, but with our lives. Calvin helpfully reminds us that it's possible, "even if [we] concern [ourselves] chiefly with [Christ]," to "stray from the right way in turning some part of [our] thinking in another direction."[3] This is a constant danger for Christians.

In life, there are many good things that demand our attention: our marriages, children, grandchildren, work, studies, sports, and cultural engagement. Yet, if we are not careful, it is very easy to forget *who* is central to everything we do—namely, our Lord

---

3 Calvin, *Institutes* 2.16.19.

Jesus. All the good things of life are fine, as long as we pursue these as a means to a larger purpose, with Christ at the centre of all that we do. For given who Jesus is and what he has done for us—and given that he is our all-sufficient Lord and Saviour who meets our every need as our great prophet, priest, and king—our only proper response is to submit ourselves to him in complete trust, love, joy, and obedience. He deserves nothing less.

How do we continue to grow in our knowledge of, love of, and obedience to Christ? First, we do so by constantly returning to his Word—namely, Scripture—for without feeding on God's Word, it is impossible to grow in the knowledge of Christ. So, we must continually study it in order to discover more about his nature, his beauty, his splendour. Scripture is foundational to knowing Christ, precisely because it is *his* Word. And to know him requires that we read and study *all* of Scripture, since his glory, person, and work can be found in all of it.

However, growing in Christ requires

more than mere knowledge *about* Christ. It is possible to study Scripture and memorise a lot of truths about God but not to know him personally. By God's grace, we must know the truth of Scripture *and also* experience our deep need of Christ. How does this occur? By the work of the Spirit, who convicts us of our sin and opens our eyes to see our desperate condition outside of Christ and the fact that we cannot save ourselves. By the work of the Spirit, who opens our eyes to the goodness of God in Christ and the merciful provision of a perfect and self-sacrificial Saviour.

Christianity is rightly described as a "sinner's religion." It's not until, by God's grace and by the convicting work of the Spirit, we come to recognise our sin before God that we gladly, joyfully, and with abiding conviction embrace Christ alone. In fact, this is the experience of every true Christian.

In my conversion, this was certainly the case. I had the privilege of being raised in a Christian home and hearing the preaching of God's Word in our local church. But this alone did not save me. In reality, although I knew a lot about the Bible and Jesus, I saw no need for him. Jesus was not precious to me. I thought I was "good" enough and not like other "bad" people. But, thankfully, by God's grace, the Holy Spirit convicted me of my sin, opened my blind eyes to see my true condition before God, and thus convinced me of my need for a Saviour. In that moment, I had no objection to Jesus as the only Saviour and Lord, because he was precisely the one I needed to rescue me from my sin and to reconcile me to himself.

As we have already discussed, Scripture clearly teaches that our greatest need as humans is to be justified before our holy, triune God. But apart from the work of the Spirit, this is something that fallen humans do not grasp. To rejoice and glory in Christ alone, then, we must first know something about our own guilt before God, our helpless condition outside of Christ, and that before God we deserve nothing but condemnation and judgement. When we know and experience this to be true, then we will gladly find our rest in Christ and the work that he finished on our behalf.

C. S. Lewis illustrates this growth in Christ in his allegorical Chronicles of Narnia series. In *Prince Caspian,* he describes an encounter between Lucy and the lion Aslan. As Lucy is lying between Aslan's front paws, looking up at him in glowing adoration, we hear this interchange:

> "Welcome, child," he said.
>
> "Aslan," said Lucy, "you're bigger."
>
> "That is because you are older, little one," answered he.
>
> "Not because you are?"
>
> "I am not. But every year you grow, you will find me bigger."[4]

Lewis has nicely captured something of how Christ becomes increasingly precious to us when we walk in him by faith. As we grow in our Christian lives through the study of

4 C. S. Lewis, *Prince Caspian: The Return to Narnia* (1951, New York: HarperCollins, 1994), 141.

Scripture and prayer, he grows bigger before us. It is important to remember that our growth in Christ is not simply an individual affair. We grow in Christ in the context of a local church. As we gather with God's people and study Scripture together, beholding Christ's beauty, Christ becomes "bigger" to us. It's not because he has changed, but because we are being transformed by the Spirit who bears witness to him. Only when we see him as he really is will we know and experience the biblical truth that Christ is all that we need in this life and forever.

May this be true of you, and may we glory in Christ alone, now and in eternity!

REFLECT or DISCUSS

1. Calvin urges believers to "drink [their] fill from this fountain, and from no other." What are some "other fountains" people often turn to for strength, security, or hope, and how can we practically cultivate a deeper dependence on Christ?
2. Why should we pursue family, work, studies, and sport "as a means to a larger purpose"? How would you describe that purpose, and what are some helps in pursuing it?
3. How can we grow in Christ? What happens as we grow?
4. How does viewing Jesus as "the jewel in the crown of Christianity" shape how you understand your faith? What are the implications?

SCRIPTURE INDEX

OLD TESTAMENT

Acts

Romans

1 Corinthians

Revelation

Also available *in the* Essentials Series

Right with God
by Michael Reeves

Scripture Is Supreme
by Tim Chester

The Trinity
by Donald Fairbairn

The New Birth
by Peter Mead

To learn more about the Essentials Series,
visit www.unionpublishing.org/essentials